THE

GIV ING

GUIDE FOR EVERY CHURCH

THE GIVING

GUIDE FOR EVERY CHURCH

USING DIGITAL TOOLS TO GROW MINISTRY

RICHARD ROGERS

FOREWORD BY J. CLIF CHRISTOPHER

Abingdon Press
Nashville

THE E-GIVING GUIDE FOR EVERY CHURCH:
USING DIGITAL TOOLS TO GROW MINISTRY

Copyright © 2016 by Abingdon Press

This book is printed on acid-free paper.

Library of Congress Cataloging-in-Publication Data

Names: Rogers, Richard, 1968- author.
Title: The E-giving guide for every church : using digital tools to grow ministry / Richard Rogers ; foreword by J. Clif Christopher.
Description: Nashville : Abingdon Press, [2016] | Includes bibliographical references.
Identifiers: LCCN 2016042403 (print) | LCCN 2016045982 (ebook) | ISBN 9781501822575 (pbk.) | ISBN 9781501822582 (e-book)
Subjects: LCSH: Christian stewardship. | Church finance.
Classification: LCC BV772 .R6235 2016 (print) | LCC BV772 (ebook) | DDC 254/.8--dc23
LC record available at https://lccn.loc.gov/2016042403

16 17 18 19 20 21 22 23 24 25—10 9 8 7 6 5 4 3 2 1
MANUFACTURED IN THE UNITED STATES OF AMERICA

Contents

Foreword

Last Christmas Eve I found myself in a church that I do not attend on a regular basis. The service was full and extremely well done. I found myself very caught up in the worship experience with great music and preaching throughout. Early on in the service one of the pastors shared how the offering for the night would be going to a mission outside the walls of this church and quickly shared that offerings could be made in a variety of ways. I admit that I was intrigued with the mission outreach the offering would be serving, but I paid very little attention to the various ways the pastor lifted up for the offering to be given. After all, I have been in the church for some sixty-four years now. I know how to do offerings. Plates will be passed, and I either drop in a check that has been prewritten for that purpose or I pull out my wallet, put money in an envelope, and drop that in the before-mentioned plate. I was going the wallet route on this night. When the time came for the offering, a short video of the mission was shown and then ushers began to pass plates. I reached for my wallet but noticed that the twenty-something young man next to me reached for his cell phone. He flipped the bulletin over to expose a QR code on the back, scanned that code with his phone, typed his gift in to the space provided, and hit send. His phone was back in its holder before the plate ever got to me.

This was an eye-opening experience. What just happened was that both of us gave to the church in the way we were both most comfortable. The gifts will get to their intended place the same, and those gifts will do just as much good. However, if this church had only offered one way to give, then one of us would not have given that night.

Churches are far behind all other nonprofits in understanding how to relate to their donors and provide ways for them to give that are most comfortable and convenient to them. In many cases they act almost like Jesus said you cannot take up any offering if it does not come from a brass plate, passed during the middle of worship, and then brought down a center aisle to be placed on the altar. No other offering will be blessed or used for kingdom work.

Richard Rogers is one of this country's foremost authorities on electronic giving. He has served the church in a variety of ways, from being a church business administrator to now serving as a vice president and consultant with Horizons Stewardship. He knows the landscape of church giving as few people do.

This book is an absolute must for church leaders to read and implement. We must get over the notion that brass plates are sacred and use every avenue available to enable persons to be comfortable in their giving. This deficit in church stewardship is one of the easiest to fix. So let's do it. Once we have set up all the various electronic means for people to be generous, then we can focus on the hard part of actually shaping their hearts to do just that.

Clif Christopher

Acknowledgments

I believe that generosity flows from a heart of gratitude, and I have often hoped to be remembered as a generous person. I am grateful to God for surrounding me with people who urge and inspire me to love God, love people, and pour my life into making disciples of Jesus Christ. I am deeply thankful to my wife, Jennifer, and our children, Ryan, Lauren, Erin, Sheridan, Jordan, Cameron, Katelyn, and Ian for the sacrifices they have made this year that allowed me to develop this resource. This book is complete because of Kristine's encouragement, ideas, and coaching and because Clif pushed me toward the finish line. I am blessed to have gifted colleagues who are also my friends. Thank you to Connie and the team at Abingdon Press for helping me get this from my head into something we hope will be useful.

Introduction

As I travel around the country working with pastors, local churches, denominational leaders, and other Christians, there is growing concern about the ability to resource vital ministry. I have yet to meet a pastor who enjoys raising money, but every single one of them understands that money equals ministry. Many churches have God-sized plans and dreams to have an impact in their neighborhood, city, state, and world. What most of them lack are sufficient resources to pursue those plans and dreams. Personally I'm not excited about raising more money for the sake of having more stuff. But when I meet Christians who want to meet a need someone has today so they can build a caring relationship with them, so they can introduce them to Jesus, so the person's life can be changed forever . . . that stirs my soul! The desire to see the next one impacted by the love of God challenges me to look for solutions, inspires me to get personally involved, and pushes me beyond my natural inclination to resist change.

After decades of involvement in the local church and experiencing how the community of faith has shaped my own marriage and the lives of my children, I've never been more excited about the opportunities facing local congregations. Today, fewer young people are connected in a vital relationship with

Jesus through a local church than we have seen in our lifetime. What a fantastic opportunity we have to BE THE CHURCH! And because I understand that in our economic system, money is the tool that allows us to do more ministry and see more lives changed I absolutely have a ball working with leaders to grow the financial base of their church. My first goal throughout the writing of this book has been to develop a resource that will help you have the money needed to achieve God's vision for your ministry. Second, I hope that your church will begin to look more and more like the Macedonian churches the Apostle Paul described in chapters 8 and 9 of 2 Corinthians. I pray that your churches will be filled with people who are generous and enthusiastically prioritize the use of their resources to build God's kingdom instead of their own.

One of the obvious ways in a digital society that a congregation can increase the number of families that are providing regular support for the ministry budget, and increase the level of support from those already participating, is through the use of electronic giving tools. The tools have become readily available and continue to improve, but I constantly hear questions and comments like these:

- How do we get started?
- What are the fees?
- Our young families don't give.
- What's the difference between an ACH, an EFT, and an e-check?

- When our members go on vacation, their summer giving goes with them.

- Do we have to accept credit cards?

- It's too expensive!

- Will our members' information be secure?

- What does "optimized for mobile use" mean?

- We don't want an ATM in our church.

- What's our next step?

- Can we use PayPal?

- We don't think it's wise to give up 3 percent in fees.

- What is a kiosk?

- Whenever we lose a Sunday for snow and ice, we lose a week of income that we never get back.

- How can we get our members to give regularly?

- We have electronic giving on our website, but nobody uses it.

- How do we increase participation?

- Are there any good service providers with whom we can partner?

- Will it integrate with our church management or bookkeeping software?

- I like to put my offering in the plate as part of my worship experience.

- What is PCI DSS?

- I gave $10 to the Red Cross in ten seconds with a text message, but I can't give digitally to my church!

These are just some of the questions and comments I hear whenever the topic of electronic giving comes up with pastors, finance committee members, stewardship teams, church business administrators, administrative councils, church staff, and board members. Questions and comments that come from a lack of good information, which, if it were available, could remove the doubt and fear that paralyze them. In my search for information to assist church leaders, I discovered an educational void in this emerging industry. The facts assert that electronic giving will profoundly impact your church's ability to resource its mission in the days and years ahead. I believe it already has.

My hope for the *E-Giving Guide* is to provide a vital tool for ministry today and to change the trajectory of resourcing for the future of your church. I want to demystify the tech and banking jargon that keeps us confused. I'll give you a resource to evaluate the costs associated with electronic giving and teach you what you need to consider when you talk to the service providers who have the tools to help you succeed. Most important, I'll help you develop a plan to begin immediately, regardless of your situation, collecting more money for ministry and missions.

For those of you who are in the discovery stages of learning about electronic giving (or you've been given this book by a friend because you're in denial), let's get started by making sure we're focused in the right place.

Why and Why *Now?*

Congregations are all unique because they are made up of unique individuals and circumstances. The geographical ministry setting and historical context shape the way a church thinks about itself and its community. Leadership styles impact the way strategic plans are implemented. Cultural and educational surroundings influence communication methods. Add to this list vast differences in population base, theological understandings, and innumerable personal preferences. We're a complex ensemble. No wonder we come in so many shapes and sizes! While none of the stories that follow are exactly the story of your church, I hope you will begin to think about yours so that you will identify what it is that your church uniquely contributes to the kingdom of God. My pastor constantly reminds us, as he prays for a different church in our community every Sunday morning, that if we are going to have the impact on our community that we want to have, it's going to take all of us. And we need all of us to have maximum impact. I've heard it called our *redemptive potential.*

First Church is 150 years old. Their history is rich with generations of families who have worshipped there; however, fewer and fewer of the younger families are continuing to be active. Those who have stayed are struggling to know if they want to continue attending a church that is still using flannelgraphs and overhead projectors. In their tech-filled lives, some of the older methods of worship, teaching, and reaching people aren't appealing. They love their families, respect their leaders, and have great memories tied to First Church. However, their children keep asking to go to the church across town with the soccer fields and the new playground. They see advertisements for VBS that look high-tech and pony rides on parents' night. The families know these things aren't what make a great church, but they know that some of their friends who they've invited to come to First Church are now active members at the other church. The First Church leaders are open to trying some new things, but their budget is very tight, as their older members have fixed incomes and their younger families don't seem to support the church financially. How are they going to update some of their programs and facilities?

Outreach Church has been focused on introducing families to the gospel and preparing them to work on the mission field for fifteen years. The nursery is continuously full, the children's ministry is serving hundreds of kids through summer programs, and the youth are taking sixty people to summer camp. A substantial majority of their active adults are involved in local missions efforts, and they have fourteen missionaries serving outside the United States. This year, two families from their membership have decided to go to Honduras to help run an orphanage. They have raised their own funds to travel, but as they plan to take their families to a remote village for a brave two-year commitment, they are giving up their homes and their income. Outreach Church wants to support these families and the orphanage. However, their missions budget is committed, and there are no extra funds that can go toward the orphanage. It's a project that has touched their hearts and aligns with their mission and vision, but they don't know how to put funds behind it.

Neighborhood Church was planted fifty years ago in a growing suburb of the Big City. Big City has continued to grow, and suburban life keeps pushing farther and farther from downtown. The neighborhood has much greater diversity than it did a few decades ago, and Neighborhood Church has a new vision for ministry and an incredible kingdom opportunity. The presence of young Hispanic families in the area has prompted several leaders to be interested in teaching ESL (English as a Second Language) classes and offering other services to the newest community members. If they could offer a Spanish-speaking service, they could fill an enormous need in their community. The administrative council agrees the timing is right for this transition. However, it would require additional resources for hiring a pastor for this segment of the congregation, development of new programs, and purchasing materials for outreach and discipleship. The field, or the neighborhood, is ready for harvest, but they don't know how to resource this great new opportunity.

Churches are facing scenarios like these all around the country. Churches of various size, age, demographics, denomination, and vision. What they have in common is their desire to "go and make disciples" (Matt 28:19). They have the right mission! The other common thread is a lack of resources to fully pursue the vision they have for accomplishing that mission. Congregations are struggling to meet budgets and secure designated funds for ministry and mission. Over and over again I hear church leaders concerned about the economy and claiming that younger members don't give to the church anymore, but it's reported that 67 percent of all households give to charity and 98.4 percent of high–net worth households give to charity.[1] The complaint about young families not giving isn't factual. However, it may be factual that they aren't giving to your church. We need to examine why. First let's take a look at the facts about the economy as it relates to generosity in America.

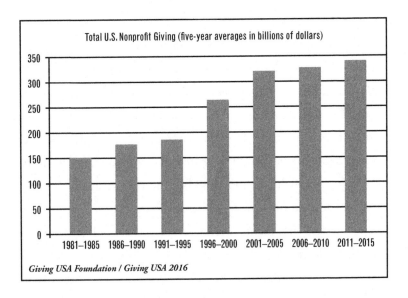

Total U.S. Nonprofit Giving (five-year averages in billions of dollars)

Giving USA Foundation / Giving USA 2016

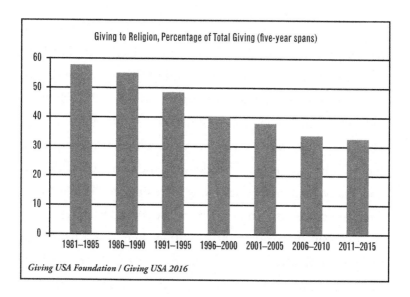

Giving to Religion, Percentage of Total Giving (five-year spans)

Giving USA Foundation / Giving USA 2016

This is not a recent discovery. In 2008, J. Clif Christopher, in his book *Not Your Parents' Offering Plate*, told us that the landscape for philanthropic giving, and particularly stewardship in the American church, had changed:

> The church used to be the predominant charity in most communities. In many, it was the only place to make a contribution of any kind. The appeal was simply, "You should give." For too many churches the appeal is still "you should give." And people respond by giving, just not to the church. They are hearing the preacher say that Jesus wants them to give, and they are choosing the youth center or the college or the hospital. Yet, our appeal is still the same.[2]

Think back to how money was collected by your church just twenty to twenty-five years ago. At the appropriate time during the worship service the ushers were asked to come forward. They stood at the front of each aisle during the prayer and then passed the offering plates up and down each row during the offertory hymn. By the end of the song the ushers had disappeared and you moved on to the next item in the bulletin. I remember wondering as a child growing up in church in the 1970s what they did with all that money piled in the offering plates. Twenty-five years later there really wasn't even enough cash in the plate to pique a child's curiosity. Checks were the currency of the day, and many churches began using envelopes to help with the counting procedures and systems of checks and balances.

Between the years 2000 and 2004 there was a handful of technological advances made that point toward the rapid rate of change America is experiencing. Facebook, the iPod, flash drives, civilian use of GPS, TiVo, hybrid cars, camera phones, and iTunes were all introduced.

Not to be left behind, the church also underwent rapid changes early in the millennium. Think back to the changes implemented in how money was collected by your church during the same time period, from 2000 to 2004. This is how it probably looked: At the appropriate time during the worship service the ushers were asked to come forward. They stood at the front of each aisle during the prayer and then passed the offering plates up and down each row during the offertory hymn. By the end of the song the ushers had disappeared and you moved on to the next item in the bulletin.

Okay, so we're not early adopters, but we are creative. As attendance and offerings decreased we started collecting prayer requests and connection cards so that it wouldn't be so easy to see the green or red fabric covering the bottom insert of the offering plate.

In the years 2005 to 2009, technology continued to change the way we American Christians—that is, consumers—lived our lives and interacted with one another and the world around us. We experienced the introduction of YouTube in 2005, the Nintendo Wii in 2006, the iPhone in 2007, the Amazon Kindle in 2008, and the Nissan Leaf in 2009.

It's a little easier to remember the changes implemented in how money was collected by your church from 2005 to 2009. For most congregations this is how it looked: At the appropriate time during the worship service the ushers were asked to come forward. They stood at the front of each aisle during the prayer and then passed the offering plates up and down each row during the offertory hymn. By the end of the song the ushers had disappeared and you moved on to the next item in the bulletin.

You get the point. If we continued this discussion into 2010 to 2014 and 2015 to 2019 it would just be more of the same. It's as if there's something nostalgic and simple about choosing never to change. "After all," they say, "we do have a website now. There's just so much change people can handle!" This attitude contributes to the slow decline in membership being experienced by so many mainline churches. Yet time seems to be speeding up. Technology and the rate of change certainly are. The resourcing challenge for churches is compounding. Not only do they have to compete for the charitable dollar, as Clif Christopher pointed out, but they also have to adjust to unfamiliar methods of collecting those dollars. The way people spend money doesn't look anything like it did at the turn of the millennium, and neither should the way churches collect it.

We weren't even talking about e-commerce in the year 2000, yet our twenty- and thirty-somethings have never experienced adulthood without it. While we are far from becoming a cashless society, our young families increasingly operate without it. A colleague of mine talks about traveling for months with the same $5 bill in his wallet because he only uses his debit and credit cards. Another friend's daughter arrived in Singapore for a visit with less than $20 cash in her purse, which she never spent or converted to local currency! When I'm speaking to a group of pastors who have traveled from out of town for a two- or three-day conference, I always ask the group for a show of hands of those who made the trip with $50 in cash. I can't remember anyone under the age of forty ever raising his or her hand . . . ever. I recently purchased my own birthday present: an Apple Watch. With my Apple Watch on my wrist, I won't even have to get out my wallet to make a purchase. By the time this book is published, I will likely be able to tithe to my church from any city, anywhere I'm working or playing, with my watch! My mind goes back to those ushers standing at the front of each aisle with hands crossed in front of them during the offertory prayer. For those of us who are older than twenty or thirty, and who grew up in the church, who would've thought that would even be possible?

To our twenty- and thirty-somethings, the language of the church, particularly around giving, can feel like a foreign language. How are they to engage in stewardship and giving when it seems no one around is speaking their language? When I was an adolescent, my father was in the army and we spent

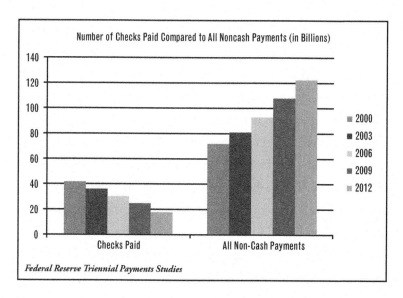

Number of Checks Paid Compared to All Noncash Payments (in Billions)

Federal Reserve Triennial Payments Studies

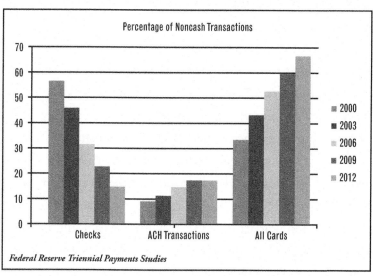

Percentage of Noncash Transactions

Federal Reserve Triennial Payments Studies

two years stationed in Germany. Living in Germany allowed us the opportunity to travel all over Europe on the weekends and summer breaks. Because each country had its own language and dialects, we simply did our best to navigate and communicate with the local people. In reflecting on this extraordinary time, I have often wondered how different it may have been had we been able to speak the local languages. What would it have been like to hear people's stories in their own words? How much richer would our experiences of their cultures have been if only we could have understood and been understood by them? Whenever I heard someone speaking English, my ears perked up, and I became eager to engage in conversation. Isn't this what we are asking of our younger generations—to try to interpret a language they do not speak?

Amazingly, churches continue to settle for passing the offering plates to younger generations of church members and regular attendees who don't speak the same language. They have come and immersed themselves into your Sunday morning worship experience. God has used the music, a testimony, and the pastor's message to stir their hearts. They have experienced the generosity of God's grace, and they want to respond, to participate. Their wallets are having a conversion experience! And they don't carry cash or a checkbook. As a result, they pass along increasingly empty offering plates. And they assume that few others support the church financially because they watch mostly empty plates passed week after week. It would be wise to start communicating in a variety of ways so that you connect with more of your congregation.

Chapter 2

Plan Your Trip

I love snow . . . when I'm on vacation in the mountains. It occurs to me that the ski trip provides a helpful metaphor for considering the use of digital tools for ministry. So I'll use it throughout the coming chapters to give you a way of visualizing this process.

My first snow skiing trip was as a teenager with a group of families from my church. It was very well organized. We (translating from the Greek phrase "My dad") just paid for the trip, packed our stuff, met at the church, and got on a bus headed for Colorado. Since then, I've taken several snow skiing vacations and learned that good planning greatly enhances the experience. The same will hold true when you introduce electronic giving to your congregation. A little planning will pay off. Group your planning into three components:

Lead, Learn, and **Launch**. Each of these three components of planning your initiative will increase its effectiveness. Each of them has individual importance, but collectively they have a compounding impact. Don't deflate your initiative by just promoting it and hoping people will get on board. While there should be some overlap in the Lead and Learn components of your plan, it's important to execute them ahead of the Launch component.

The **Lead** component is vital because it is where you are shaping the culture of the church, and that may take time and repetition. Hopefully your desire as a leader is to reflect the nature of God as a congregation. God's generosity toward us results from love and is clearly modeled in one of the most familiar verses in the Bible. John 3:16 reminds us that God so loved the world that God gave, not just a token gift, but a most precious one, the life of God's only Son. As we accept this gift, gratitude overwhelms us, and we respond through our own expressions of generosity of time, talent, and treasure. We give because God first gave. We love because God first loved. Church leaders must model the nature of God if they hope for the congregation to reflect that same nature in the community and around the world. Obviously generosity is only one aspect of God's nature, but it is an aspect that should not be ignored.

Building a culture of generosity and gratitude in your overall approach to ministry, and specifically stewardship, will provide a stronger base for electronic giving platforms. As church leaders, clergy, and laity begin to learn and communicate new ideas, remember that what you model will be valued more than what you merely say. Don't wait another day to get started!

Here are some specific ways you can **Lead** that will enhance the effectiveness of future actions:

1. Speak life into your congregation. Constantly tell them how generous they are! Remind them of the ways they

provide hope and life transformation through their generosity.

2. Develop a culture of gratitude. Thank people for serving, sharing, loving, and giving well. Celebrate what you want to duplicate! Honor faithfulness and growth in discipleship. Thank your staff. Thank your donors.

3. Share testimonies and mission-critical success stories in worship every week. Everywhere I work, faithful, committed churchgoers struggle to tell me why their church exists. I know you think they know, but they don't. The impact of your church will improve if you have a clear purpose, if people understand it, and if they see evidence of the purpose occurring. The best way to reinforce the fulfillment of that purpose is through testimonies and success stories.

> Everywhere I work, faithful, committed churchgoers struggle to tell me why their church exists. I know you think they know, but they don't. The impact of your church will improve if you have a clear purpose, if people understand it, and if they see evidence of the purpose occurring.

Leading through these culture-changing practices now will provide strategic pathways for implementing your electronic giving strategies in the near future.

The **Learn** component is going to be crucial to your plan as you communicate with other leaders and later the congregation. Some will need to better understand the need and reasons why giving patterns may vary from generation to generation within the congregation. Others will need to better understand the tools that are available and more familiar ways for people to participate financially in the accomplishment of your purpose, your organizational mission. People's need to understand something new will surface questions that you want to be prepared to answer.

Nobody I know in ministry has time to learn everything about this emerging industry, and I suspect it's going to continue to grow and change at a rapid pace. However, you want to understand the basics, be able to communicate effectively to remove barriers (fears), and have some tools that will maximize your efforts. While I'm sure it's unintentional, the banking industry, payment card industry, and electronic payments service providers often use language that is intimidating or confusing. There is a lack of consistency in the way they communicate their services and structure their pricing. Consequently, they have created barriers to the entry points that should be helping them gain customers and enable them to assist churches in improving overall resourcing. While this may be an oversimplification, let's briefly identify and define some of the technical terms and related topics you'll encounter when you begin planning your new adventure.

Glossary of Terms and Related Topics

ACH (Automated Clearing House)—an electronic banking network often used for direct deposit and electronic bill payment.[1] It is the primary system used for electronic funds transfer (EFT).[2]

automatic draft (auto-draft) authorization—a form used to enroll a donor in electronic giving using debit card, credit card, or bank (financial institution) account info

bill pay—a process initiated by donors through their bank or financial institution. Just as they do when they pay their electric bill, donors request a check to be sent to your church usually on a monthly basis.

card reader—a device that plugs into an iPad, tablet, or smartphone to capture data from a debit or credit card for making a contribution or purchase

ChMS (Church Management Software)—software designed to assist a church with managing a membership database and administrative tasks. The membership database provides an efficient way to maintain all contact information and ministry connections. Tasks typically include organizational groupings (members and guests, small group and Sunday school class affiliation, areas of service or involvement, etc.), attendance tracking, event registration, secure children's check-in capabilities, contribution data, a bookkeeping system, and often capabilities for automation of mailings, e-mails, and reporting processes. Common examples are ACS, Fellowship One, and Shelby. A current list of recommended ChMS systems can be found at www.egivingguide.com.

costs (*see* **fees**)

crowdfunding—the use of a personal fund-raising website to give a project exposure to donors outside your normal sphere of influence

donation page—the webpage connected to your church website where electronic giving transactions begin

EFT (Electronic Funds Transfer)—the electronic transfer of money from one bank account to another within a single financial institution or from one to another. This is a broad term that covers a number of payment systems, such as bill pay, direct deposit, direct debit, and wire transfers.

electronic banking *also* **online banking**—"an electronic payment system that enables customers of a bank or other financial institution to conduct a range of financial transactions" on a website operated by the institution.[3]

electronic check or e-check—other names for EFT

electronic payments service provider—a company that provides tools and services to assist a church in the collection of electronic donations and payments. A current list of recommended service providers can be found at www.egivingguide.com.

encryption—a process that provides security to data by putting it into a coded form

fees—monies charged for a service. Fees vary significantly by provider and services offered, but here's what you should ask about or expect to see:

add-on equipment and services—equipment such as kiosks and card readers that are sold or leased by companies. Some companies provide them free of charge. Depending on the business model of the service provider, there can also be a monthly fee associated with various services, such as kiosk or mobile giving options.

merchant account fees—fees that are calculated as a percentage of your dollar volume monthly and can vary significantly. Rates (called interchange fees) can vary according to the type of transaction (credit, debit, or ACH), the specific company issuing a payment card (VISA, MasterCard, American Express, Discover, etc.), and even the way a transaction is handled (card swiped or keyed in manually). Typically credit cards carry higher fees than debit cards, and ACH transaction fees are the lowest. Some service providers simplify the formula by charging an average rate based on the subscription level you have selected for their services.

setup fee—a onetime fee charged to set up your account with a service provider. When this fee exists, it is typically attributed to setting up the connection of services to your website, church management software, and any training needed to get you started.

subscription fee—an ongoing monthly fee typically attributed to ongoing services being provided. Often there are different subscription levels based on the services being used.

transaction fees—fees that are paid for each transaction that a service provider processes regardless of the amount of the transaction

group messaging service—a service that your church can use to send text messages to everyone who subscribes to your group. For instance, if you have one hundred people who "opt in" to your group, you can send a single text message that goes to all of them at once.

handheld device *also* **mobile device**—a cell phone or tablet

kiosk—"an interactive computer terminal for public use."[4] In the context of churches and electronic giving, this is a terminal set up usually in the narthex, foyer, or lobby where electronic contributions can be made on-site. The appearance and styles of these terminals vary significantly.

merchant account—"a type of bank account that allows businesses to accept payments in multiple ways, typically debit or credit cards"[5]

mobile app—a computer program "designed to run on a mobile device such as smartphones or tablet computers"[6]

mobile device *also* **handheld device**—a cell phone or tablet

mobile giving—making a financial gift through the use of a mobile device

"optimized for mobile use"—a term used to indicate that the graphics for your website or donation page have a format that is properly sized for use with a mobile device, such as a smartphone, iPad, or other tablet, when accessed by those devices. Allows for convenient, efficient access to your website or donation page.

payment aggregator—a service provider that allows merchants to accept credit card and bank transfers without having to set up a merchant account with a bank or card association. Familiar payment aggregators are PayPal and Amazon Payments.

PCI DSS (Payment Card Industry Data Security Standard) *also* **PCI compliance**—A standard created by the major credit card companies to increase security of credit and debit card-holder data in order to reduce fraud. Only the major brands (VISA, MasterCard, American Express, Discover, etc.) with the most transactions require compliance, but private-label brands may also do so voluntarily. Standards are applied at differing levels (Levels 1–4) based on the number of transactions handled. Level 1 is the highest compliance level and is required for merchants with at least six million transactions per year.

QR code (Quick Response code)—a type of barcode that is square in shape and can be read by imaging devices such as smartphones, cameras, and scanners. Used in the context of churches it serves as a link to an online form or webpage.

recurring—occurring at regular intervals (usually weekly, biweekly, semimonthly, or monthly)

screencasting—the use of a video screen during a live event to show pledges being committed toward a goal. Pledges are sent in via text message, and the results are displayed as they are occurring.

smartphone—"a mobile phone with an advanced mobile operating system. . . . [Smartphones] typically combine features of a cell phone . . . with those of other popular digital mobile devices," such as personal digital assistant, media player, and GPS navigation unit.[7] Common examples are the Apple iPhone, Samsung Galaxy, and BlackBerry.

software compatibility/integration—the ability of different types of software to communicate with each other and/or share data. This feature is one of the key criteria for selecting a service provider.

text giving—the use of a mobile phone to make a donation. Usually a keyword is sent as a text message (SMS) to a specific number (short code) and often for a predetermined amount.

user interface—the way a user interacts with the software of a computer system. It sets the tone for how the user feels about the technology, specifically how easy it is to use and how helpful it is.

website integration *also* **website branding**—the way a donation page integrates with your church website by having similar design features. Examples are the colors, layout, and presence of the church's logo.

Commit yourself and encourage your team to be conversational around the topic of electronic giving. Throughout the *E-Giving Guide* I will be responding to common questions and comments like those in the introduction. I will consistently use the terms above to help you become more comfortable with them. Come back to these definitions each time you see one of the words or phrases (in bold italics) until you've got them. One of my goals is to give your team a common language around the topic of electronic giving so you will be equipped to move forward with confidence. Start using a few of the most helpful terms above in conversations and communication with your staff, finance team, stewardship team, and congregation.

> Start using a few of the most helpful terms above in conversations and communication with your staff, finance team, stewardship team, and congregation.

This "learning period" is the best stage for vetting service providers. You will learn a lot as you talk to them, and it will also help you establish your budget to fit the way their business plan is structured. Warning: Don't get caught up in the sales pitch of the first one you talk to! They all probably do a variety of things well, and each will have unique strengths that will make them a good partner in ministry. It is imperative that you visit two or three websites of their best clients and evaluate the features you observe. I routinely make small donations on client websites to evaluate my experience and give them feedback. This would be a great way for you to test-drive one of the foundational components of any electronic giving program. If you are considering mobile giving options, then check out the mobile sites of their best clients and make a small donation. Compare what you find to what you have learned in this book and you will have a good base for making a decision.

If you are considering mobile giving options, then check out the mobile sites of their best clients and make a small donation. Compare what you find to what you have learned in this book and you will have a good base for making a decision.

Once you have begun your research and become more comfortable with the terminology of electronic giving, now is the time to formulate your plan. Remember good planning is essential for launching your electronic giving strategy. So before you hit the slopes, you will need to consider your budget, the options you will offer for electronic giving, and how you will share this news with your congregation. Just a little more preparation and then it's time to have some fun!

Develop a Quick Budget

Keep in mind that you don't have to do everything at once. There are many tools and strategies that can help you generate more money for ministry. Church leadership will need to determine how ready and adaptable a congregation is before immersing themselves in electronic giving. Your budget for launching your electronic giving initiative (or growing your participation level) will be determined by the following factors and questions your team will need to address:

1. Depending on the number of options (website donate button, giving kiosk, automatic draft authorization, mo-

bile giving, etc.) you choose to include in your electronic giving launch, you will want to consider the following:

- Do we have a website that is able to accommodate online giving?
- Is our website optimized for mobile use?
- Is our "donate" button easily seen on our website's home page?
- If we choose to use a giving kiosk(s), what style and how many will we need to purchase? Where will they be located?
- Do we have wireless Internet throughout the building? Is the signal strong enough, especially in our worship space and gathering areas?
- Do we have adequate and appropriate staffing to integrate electronic giving into our system? What training, if any, will be needed?

2. Next, you will need to review your choices for a service provider and consider the following:

- Is there a setup fee?
- Is equipment purchased or included in the subscription fee, or both?
- What other services, if any, do they provide that may further our cause?
- Is their system compatible with our church management software?
- Do they provide training and technical support for their system?

- Do they provide free marketing/promotion materials?

3. Last, you will want to be prepared to communicate these new and improved giving opportunities through all communication channels to maximize participation.

  - What are our most effective means of communication to the congregation?

  - Over what time period will we communicate our message?

  - How will we integrate live testimonies into our communication strategy?

  - How will we communicate to all members of our congregation, regardless of their familiarity with electronic giving?

  - What printed materials will we need that aren't provided by our service provider?

Budget $2-3 for each household to send a few written communication pieces to each family. More about that later. Include your setup fee for your provider and the cost of getting your website ready, if any. If you are purchasing any equipment, such as card readers or kiosks, make sure you include them in your budget.

It is likely that some of your decision makers are business-people, so it will help you to think as they do. You will want to calculate how many new giving units (based on your average giving per household) are required to break even. It is likely your budget will be covered by only a few new giving units, and the level of support from current donors is likely to increase. Providing more and better tools that make contributions to your ministry easy will soon pay dividends.

Share your e-giving strategy and initial budget with key leaders and invite their questions and comments. Conduct additional research and retool your plan, if needed. The information you need is quite accessible, so you should be able to determine your budget fairly accurately. If sufficient funds were not included in your current year's budget, here are some ways you might consider funding your e-giving strategy:

- Use appropriate designated funds.
- Invite one or a few key leaders to join you to make it happen.
- Include it in next year's budget.
- Conduct a short campaign specifically for funding this project.
- Include this project in a larger capital funds campaign.

Write Out Your Communication Plan

Before you present your ideas for approval you need to have a written communication plan for engaging the congregation with the initial rollout. Writing out your plan will force you to think about it and will also give you a more objective way to review it. I'm not saying you have to enlist a process engineer or build a Gantt chart. Just write down the key steps in your communication process, the timing of those steps, and the person responsible for each step. For multiple strategies being implemented in your initiative, break down steps unique to each strategy and combine common components. Here's an example to get you started:

Strategy	Goal	Action Step	Due Date	Responsible
ACH enroll-ment	30 new households	Clear auto-draft form with bank	Wednesday, April 1	Richard
		Introduc-tion letter writing *start w/ sample	Wednesday, April 1	Pastor
		Pulpit an-nouncement	Each Sun-day in April	Pastor
		Leader testimony	Sunday, April 12	Richard ID current enrollee
		Mailing of letter w/ return envelope	Monday, April 6	Richard
		Thank-you notes	Each Monday	Pastor
		Set up *ACH* transactions	Each Tuesday	Richard
		Celebrate total and new enrollee testimony	Sunday, May 3	Pastor and volunteer

Once you've received approval, connect with the service provider you selected and talk to them about your communication plan. Ask them for additional ideas and any resources they provide. *If there are any updates or changes to your church's website that need to be made, now is the time to get it done.* You want it to be right for people to have the best experience, before you start pointing them toward your donation page. Find three people under the age of thirty, and three people over the age of fifty to make a donation of $5 on your site. Give them a $10 gift card if they'll do it and provide you with feedback on their experience, such as:

> **Find three people under the age of thirty, and three people over the age of fifty to make a donation of $5 on your site. Give them a $10 gift card if they'll do it and provide you with feedback on their experience.**

- How was the donation made? (circle one) desktop computer, laptop, or mobile device
- Where were you? (circle one) work, home, on the go!
- Was the process fast or slow?
- Was the process easy or difficult?
- Were you ever confused or frustrated? If so, when?
- What did you like best?

Don't get too technical with your questions; just get some feedback. Talk to your website developer/designer and make the needed adjustments *before* your public push.

The **Launch** component is when you go public. Think of it as a new church-wide initiative or strategy with an aspirational goal of total involvement. Plan to promote your Launch and enroll people for an entire month with an announcement date afterward to share the results. You will be using verbal, written, and digital communication to get the word out. There are more details about your Launch month in chapter 4.

By providing good research and planning, you are giving the church a great opportunity for a successful launch into electronic giving. While it may not happen quickly, the congregation will catch on, and it will become more of the norm than the exception. You're smart enough to know that people don't just show up for a ski trip! You put in the extra work and make a good plan because you want the people you've invited to have a blast! So you've checked out your options, read reviews and reserved your accommodations, learned a little about the equipment you'll need, decided how much you can invest in the experience, made sure your friends or family know enough details to enjoy going along, and packed the vehicle. It's time to head for the mountains.

Chapter 3

Ski School

Overcoming Your Fear

I began the morning leaning on the railing of the bridge that overlooked the bunny slope where members of my family were attending ski school. My dad had offered to hang around the basin near the lodge where ski school was conducted in case any of the kids had a hard time or needed anything. I think he was actually trying to brush up on his skills so he didn't injure himself trying to keep up with the crazies in our family. Nonetheless, I found myself watching from above to make sure the instructor knew what he was doing and that we were getting our money's worth! At first I did pretty well and just listened and smiled as I saw my kids figuring it out. I'd leave and ski for a bit and then come back to check on their progress. There were many kids in the group, and the way I remember it, mine were not getting a great deal of attention or instruction. As the morning went on, I began to call out instructions to them from my perch on the bridge. Never have you seen James 1:8 better illustrated. Instantaneously my kids became double-minded, indecisive, and unstable in all their ways. Upon hearing my less-than-subtle suggestion, one of them immediately looked straight at me while executing a simple left turn, went down, and took about eight others with her. Oops.

Where Should I Start?

Everyone who shows up at a ski resort and buys a lift ticket gets to choose where he or she will start. There are many entry points to skiing: ski school, green slopes, blue slopes, black slopes, and sometimes more! You'll have many choices in the tools you use, the degree of challenge, and the terrain you're navigating. Electronic giving also has several entry points, and you get to pick where you start. For many congregations the best approach is going to be a simple one, where the risk is low and some small victories can be gained. If your church is unfamiliar with, or relatively new to, digital communication tools such as e-mail and the use of multimedia in worship services, then you'll likely want to focus first on the green-slope tools and strategies in chapter 4 as your first steps.

> If your church is unfamiliar with, or relatively new to, digital communication tools such as e-mail and the use of multimedia in worship services, then you'll likely want to focus first on the green-slope tools and strategies in chapter 4 as your first steps.

Likewise, if you are just learning the importance of an effective website, start with the recommendations in chapter 4 and spend six months to a year getting your basic systems in place.

You will need some time to polish your website, engage people in ***automatic drafts***, and get the congregation accustomed to e-mail communication from the church. Keep key leaders and influencers like your finance committee, vestry and session members, and deacons involved in your plans. Invite them to be among the first to try out new tools and provide feedback.

> **Keep key leaders and influencers like your finance committee, vestry and session members, and deacons involved in your plans. Invite them to be among the first to try out new tools and provide feedback.**

Pastors, leaders, and congregations that are more comfortable with Internet-based and electronic communication tools will be ready for a more involved launch with a variety of communication strategies and electronic giving tools like the blue-slope tools and strategies identified in chapter 5. If this is where your team is, resist the temptation to skip chapter 4. Be sure you're maximizing the opportunities available through green-slope recommendations so you keep improving your systems and exposures as you grow your base. Again, involve staff, stewardship committees, and board members as you discern the timing of next steps.

For those of you who have been at this for a while and are looking for ways to sharpen the tools you have and to add to them, you may find the earliest recommendations can help strengthen certain segments of your congregation. Your willingness to utilize a complex electronic giving initiative probably means that you understand the complex nature of a diverse congregation. Adopting the black-slope tools and strategies in chapter 6 should be done as an enhancement to strong systems already in place. You may determine that different segments in your congregation respond and engage with different tools. Of course, there will be a few pastors and leaders who ignore my advice to be a plodder and build on previous success; they will head straight for the most challenging opportunity. To them we are thankful because they provide many entertaining sermon illustrations!

Expect Resistance

As a general rule, humans resist change. Change represents the unknown, and, if given the choice, we'd rather know. This is never more obvious than in the local church. It is totally reasonable for people to have concerns about something new. We can't know for sure that anything new will lead to success or even an improvement over our current reality. The very idea of change brings out fear that gets expressed in a variety of ways. As you begin implementing an electronic giving initiative in your church, you will probably hear questions and comments that sound less than supportive: "We have electronic giving on our website, but nobody uses it." "It's too expensive." "How do we get started?" "What are the fees?" "Only young people pay bills on the Internet, and our young people aren't the ones paying the bills around here."

Pastors are going to need to be prepared to respond to statements and questions like these; however, the first thing you must resolve to do is to be fully convinced and committed yourself. Like a good ski instructor, you will need to lead by example and be familiar with what your congregation will experience when they interact with your electronic giving tools.

Pastors must champion electronic giving if they want their congregation to participate in a significant way. Pastors must be enrolled in the program and should be set up to make **recurring** gifts. Not participating would be similar to trying to lead your congregation through a transition to small groups without being in one! Or trying to convince your congregation that mission trips are life-changing experiences without ever going on one! Sounds ridiculous, doesn't it? An electronic giving initiative will not succeed without pastors believing that it will provide resources to grow ministry and talking about it from experience. The best way for you to help others overcome their fear is to have first overcome yours and then be able to share your experience.

> The best way for you to help others overcome their fear is to have first overcome yours and then be able to share your experience.

Sharing your experience takes the pressure off of you to "sell it." Make no mistake; you *will* have to promote electronic giving if you are going to lead people to participate.

Electronic giving will hopefully never be in the title of a sermon. However, sharing your experience and enthusiasm, making connections frequently during your sermons, and effectively utilizing the minute before the offering is received are all ways you can demonstrate your support. With the pastor actively supporting the initiative, leaders can now supplement what is being shared from the platform with written and digital communication and through their own participation.

As members of the church staff and governing bodies such as the administrative council, vestry, session, deacons, or lead team participate and communicate about the way they use electronic giving tools to prioritize their support for the ministry and mission of the church, involvement from the rest of the congregation will grow. Equip leaders with an FAQ sheet so they can be ready to answer common questions that will come from the congregation.

> **Equip leaders with an FAQ sheet so they can be ready to answer common questions that will come from the congregation.**

Be sure to include questions that you want people to be asking, such as one that gives you an opportunity to celebrate the growth of vital ministry that is occurring.

Church leaders can usually find reasons for why certain things won't succeed in their context, but often it's just an excuse for not putting the energy and resources into making it a priority. Trinity Episcopal Church could have let fear or tradition stand in the way of a great electronic giving initiative, but through the support and encouragement of the pastor, effective leadership has prevailed.

Success Story

Trinity Episcopal Church was founded in 1849 and sits in the heart of historic downtown Asheville, North Carolina. The parish currently has approximately one thousand members who enjoy services in their one-hundred-year-old church building. Trinity's commitment to outreach ministries in the community is historical and ongoing, beginning with building a place of worship for emancipated slaves after the Civil War, and including having an active role in founding Mission Hospital and Asheville's first public library. Today, the church continues that outreach through shelter, clothing, and food support for the homeless.

Trinity Episcopal Church defies the stereotype that seniors will not embrace electronic giving. The church financial assistant says that electronic giving makes up approximately 25 percent of the total donation plate in a parish where the average member is over the age of sixty: "Our senior members appreciate and understand how much regular donations help amortize giving throughout the year and not just during peak giving times like Christmas. A lot of members love the e-giving option."

The church has offered online giving since 2011, and what really helped it take off was support from the pastor and integrating the e-giving option into the regular pledge drive: "We are fortunate to have a highly communicative pastor who could articulate the benefits of electronic giving. We also found that personalizing an electronic giving draft form and putting it with the pledge request letter helped to speed adoption. If a member isn't able to get online to sign up, all they have to do is fill in their information and sign the form. I think the ease of being able to do things online has helped increase our cash flow. It's how people are used to paying bills. Our younger members were onboard first because they generally don't carry a checkbook with them. But our senior members have embraced it too now."[1]

Chapter 4

Greens

Getting Your Legs Under You

Have you heard of "marrying up"? It's when you find a
spouse who far exceeds your capacity. I did that. I married my best friend from college, and now we've spent over
half of our lives together. Jennifer is beautiful, smart, hilari-
ous, gifted, and generous. She's an incredible life partner, a
great mom to six children, and a successful businesswoman.
She loves God and loves people. She happens to be very strong
minded and strong willed; she is a competitor. She loves sports
and will play just about any game. While we were dating in
college she asked me to play tennis with her . . . once. I started
out playing hard, and she got frustrated and mad. I was trying to win her heart, not a tennis match, so I started volleying
easier balls back to her. It made her furious, and I was accused
of patronizing her! Pretty sure it was our first fight, and it was
definitely the only time we played tennis.

Six months into our marriage, and after a half day of ski
school on day one of her first ski trip, it was time to venture
out together. I was giddy but nervous. We got onto our first

ski lift together, and I couldn't wait for her to experience a new adventure. But I also kept thinking *tennis, tennis, tennis.* I can't remember if we got tangled up exiting the very first lift, but I can tell you it happened at some point during the day. There were several falls and a few angry tears, but she just kept getting up and I kept encouraging her. I distinctly remember the moment I thought she was done: It was late in the day, and our legs were tired. She was standing straight up and gliding along a narrow path leading to the next downhill run. Snow was falling, and the trail was full of people moving around us in tight spaces. Suddenly her feet got ahead of her, and she went down on her backside and lay back flat on the backs of her skis, knees still up, as if she were doing a sit-up. She was exhausted and didn't think she could move. The longer she lay there, the madder she got. I'm sure it was just a few moments but seemed longer. When she'd had enough of the snow landing on her cold face and people swerving to miss us, we got her back to her feet and found our way to the lodge. Exhausted and with a few new bruises, we took off our boots and outer layers of wet ski gear and began to wiggle cold fingers and toes. After some hot chocolate and exchanging highlights from the day, she admitted to looking forward to day two. We did it . . . together!

A green ski slope doesn't mean it's small. A green slope may be extremely long and take a long time to complete if enjoyed at a casual or deliberate pace. Slope ratings are not about size; they are an indication of complexity. To a skier or snowboarder, "green" indicates that the elevation change will be gradual and that there will not be unexpected obstacles. The slope will be groomed and wide. There will be plenty of room to turn for the speed you will be traveling. Slowing down and stopping will be easy for the people who are under control of their bodies and equipment. Green slopes are a great place to begin for two reasons: First, you get to see how you apply the basic skills in an environment that doesn't have a lot of risk. Second, you are introduced to variables that you can't control, such as weather conditions and other skiers, and you learn how to make adjustments, again, when your chances of not having fun are low. The hill you choose is more about complexity than size.

Knowing Your Congregation

This is also true in a church's approach to electronic giving. The size of a congregation or the size of the facilities doesn't have anything to do with the way you shape your electronic giving initiative.

> The size of a congregation or the size of the facilities doesn't have anything to do with the way you shape your electronic giving initiative.

It's more important to think about such factors as the cultural setting, congregational demographics, and current use of technology in church communications. Understanding your congregation will help you determine the complexity with which you can begin and the speed with which you can implement change. This is another reason why pastors must be completely onboard. They should have a strong sense of how quickly a congregation adapts to change and embraces technology.

If the pastor and other church leaders are new to electronic giving, then you may want to focus on doing just a few things really well. You may choose to utilize free and low-cost solutions, but it's critically important that you have easy entry points so that you have some success and realize early benefits. The following easy entry points will help you engage the congregation and implement some basic tools that will begin to stabilize annual giving (cash flow) throughout the calendar year, create new giving units, and increase support from some of your current contributors.

"Click Here"

This is a good time to reiterate that your website matters, a lot. Your "Giving" button or menu option should be prominent. It should be located in the upper right corner of your website home page and should also be a different color than the other items competing for attention. It doesn't have to be flashing or an obnoxious, fluorescent color. It can be a complementary color to the rest of the home page, but it needs to be unique and draw the user's eye to its direction. Selecting the "Giving" button will navigate a person to a ***donation page*** that should have design features similar to the rest of the church's website.

Donors have higher confidence when they don't feel like they are being sent to a third-party site to handle their contribution. They trust the church and want to make a gift but may not have that same confidence with an outside company. At the very least, make sure your church's name and logo are prominent on the ***donation page***. An enhancement would be to use a consistent color scheme also. If your strategy is to keep it simple, then you want to make sure that it is very easy—with very few steps—to make a gift. Always personalize the message in the e-mail that is automatically generated when someone makes an online gift. It should be a genuine, heartfelt expression of gratitude from the pastor and should reiterate that the gift supports the incredible work being done by the church to change lives. Here are a couple of examples:

> Michael, thank you for your gift to Hill View Church. This summer we had eighty-three children participate in vacation Bible school and also a total of forty-two youth and adults working on three different mission projects in our community. We've already seen six children and thirteen adults in our town make decisions to accept Jesus as their Savior this year! Generous gifts like yours enable us to do more ministry and see lives changed. Thank you again for making a difference. —Pastor Mark

> Thank you for your $500 gift to the Building Fund of First Church. We are celebrating our sixtieth year of "Making Disciples of Jesus Christ for the Transformation of the World," and we are expecting our greatest year ever! More people are connected to a small group than at any time in our history, and our children's and youth ministries are bursting at the seams. The renovation and expansion of our Christian education space couldn't come at a better time. Thank you for investing in our future. —Rev. McMurray

ACH Transactions

One of the best "green slope" strategies is to utilize *automated clearing house (ACH)* transactions, which are often free if the church is the one doing the legwork. They are extremely easy to set up. All you need is an *auto-draft authorization* form and an introduction letter like the samples on pages 47–48.

You may also download these free resources from my website www.egivingguide.com or view them on your *smartphone* by scanning this *QR code*:

Here are the steps you'll want to take to implement this part of your e-giving program:

1. Take the *auto-draft authorization* form to your church's bank/financial institution and tell them you plan to give people the option of making direct payments from their personal accounts to the church on a *recurring* basis.

2. Show them the form and see if they require any additional information or if they have their own version they'd like for you to use.

3. Confirm/negotiate the terms/cost of these transactions. Typically banks do not charge a fee for these transactions when they have the church's other accounts.

Auto-Draft Authorization

I (we) hereby authorize (***insert church name), hereinafter called CHURCH, to initiate debit entries to my (our) account indicated below and the financial institution named below, hereinafter called FINANCIAL INSTITUTION, to credit the same to such account. I (we) acknowledge that the origination of ACH transactions to my (our) account must comply with the provisions of U.S. law.

Account Information

_____

(Financial Institution Name)   (Branch)

_____

(Address)   (City/State)   (Zip)

Type of Acct: ____Checking ____Savings

_____

(Routing Number—9 digits)

_____

(Account Number)

_____   _____

(Amount)   (Frequency)

This authority is to remain in full force and effect until INDIVIDUAL notifies CHURCH of termination of debit entry.

_____   _____

(Print Individual Name)   (Signature)

_____   _____

(Print Individual Name)   (Signature)

                                _____

                                (Date)

TO HELP US WITH ACCURACY, PLEASE INCLUDE A COPY OF A VOIDED CHECK WITH THIS FORM!

Dear Fred and Susan,

I can't believe we are just a few weeks away from the start of Vacation Bible School. This ministry has had an incredible impact not only on the families at (our church), but also the families of (our city). Just last year we had sixty-three children participate and another thirty-five adult and youth volunteers. Sixteen of these children did not previously have a church home and seven of them have now joined the church with their families. The greatest news from VBS last year is that we had six children begin a relationship with Jesus! We already have more kids preregistered this year, and we are anticipating our best VBS ever!

(***Segment the following paragraph to the group with whom you're writing)
The generosity of our congregation makes this possible. I'd like to invite you to participate financially in the life-changing ministries of (our church) and we've made it easier than ever before.
(or)
Your financial generosity makes this possible. We've made it easier than ever to make regular contributions to (our church) and stabilize cash flow during the summer months when families typically take time for vacation.
(or)
Many families prioritize (our church) in their regular giving. This faithfulness allows us to maximize the impact of many life-changing outreach efforts like VBS. I appreciate the commitment of your family to help us connect people to a loving God.

Enclosed is an Auto-Draft Authorization form that you can use to make your gifts to (our church) happen every week or month automatically. All we need is a little information about you and your bank, along with the amount and frequency of your gift, and we can set it up for you. Use the return envelope provided for your convenience. You may discontinue this service at any time by contacting _____ in the church office at (XXX) XXX-XXXX.

If you prefer to set up an online gift using a debit or credit card, use your smartphone to scan the QR code below and it will guide you through a few easy steps on our website.

Thank you for helping us "reach the next one."

Pastor

4. Ask your bank *how* and *when* they will provide reports reflecting these transactions so that you may track contributions for your donors.

5. Once you have arrangements confirmed with your bank, draft an introduction letter that will be mailed/e-mailed with the ***auto-draft authorization*** form. I suggest that you always consider different groups who will be receiving these letters and make sure the message matches the group. Examples of groups may be non-givers, new pledging units, all pledging units, people currently making regular donations with credit and debit cards, people who give irregularly but consistently with their attendance patterns, senior adults, young adults, and so on. The sample adaptable letter included is a good starting point.

6. Be specific about what you're asking them to consider and how they can take action right now.

7. Enclose a return addressed #9 envelope with your mailing address to encourage an immediate response.

Strategic Variations

e Remember your groups when deciding *how* you will distribute this request. If your church has an active database of the congregation's e-mail addresses and you regularly communicate through e-mail, an e-mail link directly to your ***donation page*** to set up a ***recurring*** gift is a better (or additional) option. A word of caution: Don't assume that these families are the only ones who will participate in electronic giving. Absolutely use written communication to connect with families for whom you don't have a current e-mail address. If in doubt, use both!

e Another option would be to include a ***QR code*** (linking to your ***donation page***) at the bottom of the introduction letter to give them two options for participating in electronic giving. Smartphone users will be very comfortable with this tool and will likely set up the contribution for you!

e Once you are set up with your bank and have a system in place, you can add a checkbox on your annual pledge card (like the sample shown on the next page) with a note to include a voided check and a simplified version of the ***auto-draft authorization*** form on the back of the pledge card. Once again, adding a ***QR code*** on your pledge card will expedite the process for some families and enhance efficiency for your staff.

Whenever the church office receives an ***auto-draft authorization*** form from a contributor, a thank-you note should be sent immediately from the pastor, and the ***recurring*** transaction should be set up with the financial institution. Since the church is saving money by setting these transactions up without the aid of an ***electronic payments service provider***, the financial secretary will use the report provided by the bank to manually post contributions just as they would any regular offering donation.

Because I/we love our church and are committed to impacting lives, I/we pledge to the [year] ministry budget:

Total 1-year commitment for January–December: $_____

This pledge may be revised should circumstances make it necessary.

☐ I/We would like you to draft a checking account monthly. *(Please complete form on back of card.)*

☐ I/We will regularly give by check, cash, and/or credit card. *[church website donation page]*

"You will be made rich in every way so that you can be generous in every way. Such generosity produces thanksgiving to God through us."

2 CORINTHIANS 9:11 CEB

Your name(s) _____ Address: _____

City: _____ State: _____ Zip: _____ Phone: _____

E-mail: _____

Signature(s): _____ Date: _____

Authorization of Direct Pay for [Year] Ministry Budget

I/We_____ hereby authorize [church name] to draft

$_____ /month from the following bank account:

Bank name:_____ Please attach voided check from account to be drafted so bank information can be verified.

Routing # (9 digits):_____ Account #:_____

This authorization is to remain in force and effect until [church name] has received written notice from me (or either of us) of its termination in such time and manner as to afford [church name] and depository a reasonable time to act on it. Payment will occur on the 15th of each month.

Signature(s): _____

Payment Aggregator

Another strategy for those wishing to keep it simple is to use a ***payment aggregator*** like PayPal or Amazon Payments. The ***fees*** are reasonable, and these companies have significant trust and brand recognition. It is likely that the members of your congregation who would consider making an online contribution already have an account set up with one of these companies. Like the ***ACH transactions*** above, the only downside to these transactions is that you will have to manually enter them into your church software system in the same way that you enter gifts of cash and checks. It's never bad to have

51

contributions to post, but there are tools we'll discuss later that can simplify that process if you choose to use them.

Pastor Involvement

Regardless of church size or the complexity of your electronic giving program, the pastor will have to champion the effort if you hope to maximize participation. This is not just a good idea; it is an essential strategy for this initiative.

> Regardless of church size or the complexity of your electronic giving program, the pastor will have to champion the effort if you hope to maximize participation.

"If the pastor believes in it, that's the lynchpin!" says Marty Baker, pastor of Stevens Creek Church and founder of SecureGive.

Pastors should enroll as users in the church's electronic giving program and make *recurring* gifts. They will be the primary spokespeople as they share about their involvement and invite others to give electronically.

The Offering

The time leading up to or during the offering is one of the most missed opportunities in the church. Many of our greatest supporters gather weekly throughout the year, which makes us the envy of every other nonprofit. Fifty-two weekends a year we get to ask for support of our mission and ministries. The words shared during these brief moments should be used strategically and should never be disconnected from discipleship. Woven into stories of changed lives there should be threads of families who give *recurring* electronic gifts. Connected to a pastor's expression of gratitude in a story of impact there should be a reminder of how easy it is to prioritize this area of discipleship through electronic giving and reach the next one for Christ. Along with sharing a Bible verse that expresses gratitude or generosity, you can add a word of instruction for enrolling in electronic giving. Here's an example:

> As we were reading today in Luke 12:34 about our hearts following our treasure, I was overwhelmed with gratitude by the generosity of our congregation. There is no question that many of us have aligned the desires of our heart with the ministry of this church. It is obvious by the way you give faithfully to see people's lives changed forever by the grace of God. Jillian, whom many of you met for the first time today, is a recent example of the impact you are having on this community. Thank you!

You will find a list of great ideas for your offering communication at www.egivingguide.com.

Launch Date

An effective way to build enthusiasm is to utilize a Launch Date when you will begin enrolling families in electronic giving. You should promote this initiative for at least four weeks so you catch those who attend worship services at least once a month. Use your worship bulletin, newsletter, announcements, an e-mail blast, and include the dates in your introduction letter. If you have had electronic giving options for some time and want to renew interest or increase participation, use a ReLaunch approach and highlight new tools or new features of your website to build interest.

Use a response card in all worship services for four weeks beginning with your Launch or ReLaunch Date. All you need is something simple to provide a way for people to express interest or, even better, a way for them to enroll. A card like the one pictured here can be adapted to fit your needs. Make it easy!

Electronic Giving **at Your Church**

☐ I would like to give electronically.
   Please send me more information.

☐ I already give electronically.

Your name _____

Phone _____

E-mail _____

Some church leaders wait until they have a problem to try to address it. Most of us prefer to stay in our comfort zone until we get pushed out of it. Thankfully there are leaders who don't wait to get pushed! Hillspring Church anticipated the benefit of having a congregation that utilizes *recurring* gifts through electronic giving, and their willingness to change before it was comfortable might have saved their budget.

Success Story

Hillspring Church is obsessed with their mission of *Making a Difference . . . Together!* They use their resources to reach people with the gospel of Jesus Christ and invite them into a life-changing relationship. They are committed to connecting with people through inspiring worship, relevant preaching, and sacrificially serving under-resourced people in Oklahoma and around the globe. Each year they see hundreds of people make commitments to follow Christ.

Hillspring Church now has two campuses: in Sand Springs and Owasso, Oklahoma, but things certainly haven't always been easy. In 2011 the Sand Springs campus was the only campus. Staff offices were in portable buildings in the parking lot, the welcoming space was cramped, and the children's space was completely inadequate. After a failed earlier attempt to raise the money on their own, church leaders made a bold decision to hire a consultant and conduct a capital campaign. The winter of early 2014 brought snow and ice storms to the Tulsa area on six different weekends. On three Sundays, services had to be canceled because no one could get to church safely. Fortunately, church leadership had been promoting online giving through the church's website and worship services for a few years, and Hillspring was collecting 29 percent of all operating income through ***recurring*** electronic gifts. By July, in the third year of a capital campaign, Hillspring Church was ahead of schedule on the fulfillment of campaign commitments *and* was running an operating budget surplus!

Blues

Building Confidence and Competence

Meet you at the bottom of the lift," said one of my teenagers as we gathered at the top of a string of blue slopes we'd been skiing and snowboarding for the past hour or two. There was an immediate understanding within the group of novice but growing-in-confidence skiers: the phrase "Meet you at . . ." really meant "Race you to . . . ," and by the time I had adjusted my goggles I was standing alone on the small plateau that had just become a launch point. As bad as it is to be the aging dad with three prior knee surgeries and a bad back, trying to keep up with my oldest three, there is a built-in advantage to being 225 pounds with gravity and longer skis working in your favor. I have also been snow skiing several more times than my children so I have an advantage in experience and judgment. Simply put, I have better tools for this exercise than they have, but sprinting off the starting line like my hair is on fire isn't one of them.

You've heard the expression "slow and steady wins the race"? Slow and steady can turn into a lot of momentum once you get movement and don't interrupt it. I'm certainly not an expert, but I've been on the mountain enough to know to keep my skis parallel, stay relaxed so I don't fatigue too quickly, keep my knees bent, and keep my eyes looking well ahead of me so I can anticipate what is coming and "maintain a good line." At this age, my girls were brand new to skiing and had a healthy desire to avoid getting injured. Too much speed scared the younger one, and she was more motivated to survive than to win. She was weaving back and forth, falling occasionally and lacking trust in her training. She really wasn't utilizing the basic tools available, and I passed her quickly. Her older sister is fiercely competitive but can get frustrated by a setback and prolong the accomplishment of a goal because she gets tense. She has extremely high expectations of herself yet doesn't always give herself the grace to learn at a reasonable pace. It took me much longer to catch her because of her sheer determination to beat me. Eventually her technique and inexperience let her down and she would have to slow down to regain her balance or stand up straight to rest her tiring legs. She had the right tools to succeed but hadn't applied them consistently and long enough to achieve the result she desired.

Then there's my son, the most competitive person I've ever met. He would rather suffer an injury trying to win, than finish safely in second. He's very emotional, and all that energy can work for him or against him. When it's going well, you might as well learn to lose graciously because you won't beat him. But if he starts to doubt himself, it can get ugly in a hurry. I have failed to mention that some of my family enjoys trash talking. Mainly it's me, but it's a skill I've endeavored to pass down. In desperate times, like when a child is about to defeat a parent in a game of skill, you do what you need to do in order to help him grow in character (or something like that). As soon as I thought he could hear me, I made sure he knew I was gaining on him. First he started checking my position and then began to worry that I was catching him. He lost his focus. Little miscalculations turned into mistakes that helped me close the gap quicker. Pointing them out and getting him flustered sealed it. He had the tools, but he abandoned them by getting distracted!

Blue ski slopes can be an entry point to skiing or something that a beginner works up to. They would be considered "intermediate." There are several reasons a slope might have a blue rating. It will have a steeper slope than a green and may have sections where you have to work to control your speed. It may also have obstacles or changes in the terrain. Some blue slopes have small moguls (bumps), and most will provide opportunities to get off the main path and navigate trails through trees or areas that are not groomed and may have deep powder. If you've learned the basics of skiing and can control your equipment, blue slopes may be right for you. They are more challenging and can be a little intimidating to the beginner. Success on blue slopes will come not only because you have the mental and physical tools necessary but also because you are applying the tools consistently over time. Blue slopes are more rewarding to finish and are definitely more fun!

For the church that is not facing barriers to or intimidated by electronic giving, an intermediate approach will help you have greater success in a shorter amount of time. This is possible because you are increasing exposures and using more tools than you would with a beginner approach. Similar to skiing, being an intermediate also requires greater commitment.

> For the church that is not facing barriers to or intimidated by electronic giving, an intermediate approach will help you have greater success in a shorter amount of time.

Master the Basics

A church can work up to or even begin with these tools, but you absolutely must utilize some of the foundational tools from chapter 4. Every church that is serious about effectively using electronic giving to increase resources for ministry and mission should have regular enrollment opportunities for *ACH* transactions. Even if you are using an *electronic payments service provider* to handle your *ACH* transactions, the *fees* are typically lower than debit card and credit card transactions. While many credit card users like to earn points or rewards with their transaction activity, debit card users are easy to convert to *ACH*. Once or twice a year, contact the families who make *recurring* debit card donations and ask them if they'd like for you to set it up as an *ACH* transaction for them.

> Once or twice a year, contact the families who make *recurring* debit card donations and ask them if they'd like for you to set it up as an *ACH* transaction for them.

Another tool from chapter 4 that is essential at this stage is that the pastor must personally be using and promoting the electronic giving tools available. Additionally, church leadership should be using the messaging shared around the offering time during worship services strategically to encourage *recurring* electronic gifts.

"Optimized for Mobile Use"

Everything I said about your website in the last chapter is nonnegotiable for a church that is serious about growing participation in electronic giving. I wish I had a dollar for every time I've heard a person over forty years old say something like, "Our young families don't give." If you are planning to engage younger members and attenders and disciple them in the stewardship of their financial resources, then you will need to take your website another step up and ensure that it is *optimized for mobile use*. This is not expensive and is essential if you desire the participation of young people. Blackbaud reported that 17 percent of all online gifts made on Giving Tuesday, December 1, 2015, were made using a *mobile device*, which was an increase of more than 30 percent from the previous year. Steve MacLaughlin, director of analytics at Blackbaud, reported that charities with mobile-friendly websites and *donation pages* can attract more gifts.[1] Increasing numbers of people are mobile-phone users. People are experiencing your church website on a *mobile device*, and they simply won't tolerate having to shrink, expand, scroll, and search around a page that is not *optimized for mobile use*. If you insist on making it difficult, they will leave . . . with their gift.

Recurring Gifts

Recurring, recurring, recurring—the greatest characteristic of electronic giving opportunities is the *recurring* gift. If you would like to have a substantial percentage of your income coming to you through regular, consistent gifts to stabilize cash flow throughout the ministry year, *recurring* electronic gifts (donations, transactions, whatever you want to call them) are the way to accomplish it.

Every church that is launching an electronic giving initiative should use an appropriate variation of the Introduction Letter and *auto-draft authorization* (from chapter 4). Most churches that already have an electronic giving program would also increase participation through an intentional effort that includes this correspondence. This would be a great excuse to remind people of how their stewardship or generosity is making an impact through their church.

Electronic Payments Service Provider

If you are considering blue-slope tools and strategies, you should partner with an *electronic payments service provider*. Each of them has different strengths, so the more you know about the industry and your situation, the easier it will be to identify the *service provider* that will be the best fit for your church. While it should be one of the factors you consider, the cost of services should rarely be the deciding factor. The variety of tools and services they provide, communication strategies, *user interface*, and software features and compatibility should all be considered. This *service provider* will also have a very good understanding of current security compliance regulations. They should be able to provide you with frequently asked questions (FAQs) and understandable responses to share with the congregation. Although you may not have a grasp of *PCI DSS*, it's good to have a *service provider* that does.

> One of the major advantages of using some *electronic payments service providers* is the ability of their software to integrate or communicate with your *church management software.*

As an aside, remember that all data entry has a cost. Whether your church bookkeeper is using pencil and ledger paper, personal computer software that was designed for small business applications, or *church management software* that is designed for churches, all data entry costs something. Sometimes the most significant costs are inefficiency and inaccuracy. One of the major advantages of using some *electronic payments service providers* is the ability of their software to integrate or communicate with your *church management software.* This feature can automate the posting of electronic contributions, saving the church bookkeeper time and potential mistakes. Use the following table to note the similarities and assess the unique features of the *service providers* you consider:

	Provider 1	Provider 2	Provider 3
Will service integrate with our church management software? If so, how?			
Can they "brand" or customize donation page to match the look of the church website?			
User interface (what did people say who tested it?)			
How is reporting of contributions received?			
How quickly do we have access to contributions?			
Merchant contract required?			
Services available: (check each)	Online giving Mobile giving Text giving Kiosk giving Accept ACH Debit only (option) Accept pledges	Online giving Mobile giving Text giving Kiosk giving Accept ACH Debit only (option) Accept pledges	Online giving Mobile giving Text giving Kiosk giving Accept ACH Debit only (option) Accept pledges

(continued)

	Provider 1	Provider 2	Provider 3
	Accept payments Event registration Personal messages Website design Support Multi-site Other:	Accept payments Event registration Personal messages Website design Support Multi-site Other:	Accept payments Event registration Personal messages Website design Support Multi-site Other:
Setup Fee?			
Plans Offered: (show monthly fee and interest rate)	A) B) C) D)	A) B) C) D)	A) B) C) D)
ACH Rate?			
Equipment Cost/Fee			

This free resource may also be downloaded from www .egivingguide.com. On the site you will also find a listing of **electronic payments service providers** that I'm recommending. If the **electronic payments service provider** that you select has tiered plans offering different rates based on transaction volume, you can run a cost analysis to determine the breakeven point for moving from one plan to another. There is a tool on the website to help you with this also.

Blue-slope tools and strategies are intentional efforts to increase exposures to your electronic giving initiative and provide a variety of tools through which people can participate. Besides optimizing your website for mobile use there are more ways to accomplish these two things.

QR Codes

Instruct *smartphone* users to download a free *QR code* reader app from their *mobile app* store. Then use a *QR code* to link them to your *donation page* (where you will make sure they have the option of choosing a *recurring* gift). There are websites that will generate a free *QR code* that you can download and use in all print media communications. This *QR code* with a brief sentence inviting people to scan it with a *smartphone* should be inserted into your electronic giving enrollment letters and cards, the weekly worship bulletin, annual pledge cards, capital campaign pledge cards, contribution statements, and seat back cards.

Seat Back Cards

Use seat back (pew pocket) cards to promote electronic giving and provide people a way to participate in worship. This simple tool has many benefits:

1. Allows electronic giving users to participate in the weekly offering, reinforcing the message that our congregation is generous

2. Provides electronic giving users a discipleship tool for teaching their children to tithe

3. Models the act of giving for those who are new to the congregation

4. Creates curiosity among those not yet involved in electronic giving

5. Provides easy instructions for enrolling with an immediate way to respond

The seat back cards should be durable or laminated so they may be collected from the offering plates or buckets and restocked for use the following week.

Kiosks and Card Readers

Utilize one or more giving *kiosks* or *card readers* in the highest-traffic areas adjacent to where worship services are conducted. Regardless of whether you place it in your narthex or foyer or the gathering space for your coffee shop, you can find a style of **kiosk** or **card reader** that fits the culture of your church. Churches using these digital giving tools are providing their congregation with a way to give that is increasingly common and comfortable. As shown in chapter 1, the use of debit and credit cards is on the rise. If church leadership is uncomfortable with the congregation using a credit card to make a gift to the church, make sure your **electronic payments service provider** will give you the option of accepting debit cards only.

> If church leadership is uncomfortable with the congregation using a credit card to make a gift to the church, make sure your *electronic payments service provider* will give you the option of accepting debit cards only.

I've often heard a comment that goes something like this: "We don't want an ATM machine in our building." My first response is that **kiosks** and **card readers** come in many shapes, sizes, and styles. Sometimes I add that I don't use one for regular offerings either, because I already have my tithe set up to be given automatically every week to help the church with steady cash flow throughout the year. Then I also add that I have seen people at the end of a worship service waiting in line to use a **kiosk** or **card reader.**

I have a friend who attends a multisite church in Arkansas, and he loves to travel around the state during the summer to go camping. He and his wife often stay near a community that has one of the church campuses so that they can attend church in a familiar environment even when they are on the road. He recently asked me if I knew we had a giving *kiosk* at our campus. Then he told me that while he was at another campus the previous weekend he had left his phone in his car during church because he's always afraid he'll forget to silence the ringer. He was reminded during the offering time that many families make their weekly gift electronically and the ways for doing so were listed. After the service ended, he walked out of the worship center and looked for a giving *kiosk, stood in line,* selected his home campus on the *kiosk* menu, and was able to make his regular gift from another city, without his cell phone! I wasn't sure what to be more excited about, his determination as a disciple or his church's intentionality in making them.

Just because *you* have a hang-up about something, don't assume everyone else does as well. If your congregation is slow to adjust to changes in technology, you can utilize some of the other software features on a *kiosk* to give people time to get accustomed to this tool before activating electronic giving options. Use your *kiosk* for small group signups or VBS registration or for collecting prayer requests for several months and then activate giving options around a Launch or ReLaunch as discussed in chapter 4.

> If your congregation is slow to adjust to changes in technology, you can utilize some of the other software features on a *kiosk* to give people time to get accustomed to this tool before activating electronic giving options.

Printed Communications

Utilize print communication channels to increase partici-pation in electronic giving. Here are some ideas:

- Periodically post a fact or share a story related to elec-tronic giving in the church newsletter to remind the congregation about the tools that are available.

- Share a testimony of a family that has used electronic giving to prioritize their giving in the ministry update mailed with your quarterly contribution statements.

- Include a return envelope and an electronic giving enrollment form and/or your **QR code** linked to your **donation page** with every contribution statement from the church.

- Utilize the back of your annual operating pledge cards or capital campaign commitment cards to include an enrollment form and your **QR code.**

- Place a sentence expressing gratitude to your generous congregation and include your **QR code** in the worship bulletin.

- Print the back of your offering envelopes with a graphic showing the various ways to give to the church, which includes electronic options.

*Whenever using a **QR code**, include a brief word of instruc-tion; don't just stick it in there.*

Digital Communications

Utilize digital communication channels to increase participation in electronic giving. Here are some ideas:

- Create a graphic that shows the various options for financially supporting the mission and ministries of the church and scroll it with other announcements on television or video screens throughout your facilities.
- Utilize a mass e-mail service to invite people to participate in the electronic giving initiative. Embed a video from the pastor expressing appreciation and sharing about personal involvement, how easy it was to enroll, and the specific action point you're asking them to consider. Don't forget to include a link to your ***donation page!***
- If your church has a Facebook page, consider adding their "Donate Now" button that nonprofits can put on their pages linking to their ***donation page.***
- I've already mentioned this in chapter 4, but I've seen so many bad examples that it's worth repeating: *Always* personalize the message in the e-mail that is automatically generated when someone makes an online gift. It should be a genuine, heartfelt expression of gratitude from the pastor and reiterate that the gift supports the incredible work being done by the church to change lives.

It's generally a good idea to be self-aware and build upon your strengths. Arguably we spend too much time trying to shore up our weaknesses, aspiring to be adequate in all our endeavors. Frustratingly, we're not equipped with gifting or a passion for many of the things we attempt. No individual, organization, or church is going to be great at everything. Most churches I've observed are trying to do too many things, and the result is that they struggle to do anything with excellence. As you grow your church's involvement in electronic giving, make sure you're doing a few things really well before experimenting with the next great idea that comes along. A system produces what it is designed to produce. Churches with focused leadership work to design effective systems and then work their systems, observing the wise adage, "Plan your work and work your plan." Acts 2 United Methodist Church hasn't experimented with every digital tool for growing resources, but they have been laser focused on growing *recurring* gifts and making it extremely easy to give and make other financial transactions related to their ministry.

Success Story

Acts 2 United Methodist Church has strong leadership that seems determined not to be distracted. Since the time founding pastor Mark Foster and the Oklahoma Annual Conference decided to plant and support a new church in the growing suburbs north of Oklahoma City, the dream has been "to create a people who sing God's praises, serve God's children, and share God's salvation until Christ comes again."

The area is full of young families, and the church is a reflection of the community. The average age among member families in the church is thirty-one. Yes, thirty-one. Acts 2 UMC doesn't try to do every ministry needed in their growing community, but they focus their energy and resources on reaching and equipping young families and children. Neither do they try to utilize every electronic giving tool at their disposal, but they have been very effective with the tools and strategies they've used.

They began by promoting **ACH** transactions and having an ***electronic payments service provider*** handle those transactions. The congregation was invited to participate, and the staff initiated the *recurring* transactions for the participants. In 2014, the church added online giving through their website, and by the end of the year, 10 percent of total giving and 13 percent of general fund giving had been received electronically.

By the end of 2015, the church had experienced even greater balance to monthly income through *recurring* gifts. Forty-four percent of total giving and 51 percent of general fund giving came outside the offering plate through electronic giving.

The keys have been ease of use and consistency in keeping electronic giving options in front of the congregation. The church website is ***optimized for mobile use***. Electronic giving options are made known in every worship service. Invitations to utilize **ACH** transactions are made during every pledge campaign. A **QR code** linking potential users to the donation-landing page of the church website is on the back of the bulletin every week. Debit cards can be used at a ***card reader*** to pay for nondeductible transactions such as camp fees, small group resources, VBS T-shirts, and CDs. In a nutshell, they make it easy and they make it obvious.

There is little doubt that Acts 2 UMC will add to the ways their congregation can participate financially in the ministries and mission of the church, but assuredly the new strategies will be built on existing strengths and be driven by their dream.

Chapter 6

Blacks

Using Your Edges

R ambo." "Black Hole." "Delirium Dive." "The Cliff."
"Straight Shot." "Kill the Banker." "So Long." "The Bite."
"Eclipse." "The Wall." "Outer Limits." "Hemlocks." "Barry
Barry Steep." These are names of well-known black slopes.
I'm fairly certain that when selecting names, resort owners try
to scare intermediate skiers away from the most challenging
slopes. Seems reasonable to me.

It was day four of the first ski trip with my wife—yes,
the same woman who was lying on her back in a sit-up position and crying just three days earlier. It was the final run of
a great week of skiing, and I talked her into trying the short-
est route down to the lodge. She'd overcome fears, learned the
basic maneuvers, gained confidence, mastered her turns, and
had lots of fun. She was feeling up to the challenge, and we'd
worked our way down to the last segment. As we approached a
plateau the mountain seemed to disappear in front of us, and
we slowed to a stop beside a group of indecisive admirers. The
sign said "Go Devil" and there was a black diamond beside the

75

name. In our assessment a more appropriate name had never been given. As we stood there looking down, seemingly straight down, Jennifer mumbled that you'd have to be possessed by the devil to want to take this route. Or maybe she said that she'd married the devil, but it's difficult to recall because I started having another tennis date flashback. Anyway, I lied and told her that I knew she could do it. I'm pretty sure that she wanted to try. We talked through a plan, and she began working her way down the steep slope. I stayed behind her, cheering her on and reminding her to stay on the edges of her skis and keep her weight leaning up the hill as she crossed the narrow passageway from side to side.

As she got to the last one hundred yards, and with me at a safe distance behind her, she turned her skis straight toward the lodge and shot down the mountain, raising her hands in victory as the ground leveled. She quickly turned both skis to her left and leaned hard to stop, spraying powder everywhere. Watching her and seeing that smile below her goggles was the highlight of my trip! The way she tells the story is that we were racing down the mountain and she had won.

It's certainly not the point of this chapter to get you thinking that black slopes are all scary and dangerous and should be avoided. Similarly, the less common tools or more complex electronic giving strategies shouldn't be left solely to the experts, but church leaders will want to make sure these tools and strategies are the right step at the right time. They are grouped together in this chapter because you can have fantastic electronic giving participation without them, but they can also enhance what you are doing in a significant way if they are properly used.

Screencasting

A good example of a tool that is an "extra" but can be utilized very effectively in the right situation is *screencasting*. Screencasting leverages the energy and enthusiasm of a large group gathering that has a celebratory vibe to encourage participation in a fund-raising effort. This is an online service that allows you to track and monitor pledges during a live event. A goal is set and is displayed on video monitors or a projection screen. Participants in the live event are invited to text in a pledge, and the progress is updated in real time. A good application for this technology might be a missions banquet or a youth fund-raiser that requires significant support from adults in the church.

Group Messaging

Use a *group messaging* service to send occasional text messages to the congregation, including content or a link once each calendar quarter that is related to electronic giving. One example is sending a sentence expressing gratitude for the generosity of the church following a financial need in the congregation that was met. Another example is sending an enthusiastic sentence about the upcoming electronic giving initiative Launch with a link to the *donation page*. Encourage them to be one of the first new families to enroll!

Text Giving

Nonprofits have been using *text giving* in disaster relief efforts for years. Give people an easy way to respond immediately to an urgent or compelling need. Since *mobile device* use continues to grow, it makes sense to leverage a portable tool for generosity. Churches can use *text giving* in a variety of circumstances. Promote it alongside your regular giving options during the offering so people who give spontaneously, or only when they attend worship, can participate. Also use this method for special offerings like a First Fruit Offering during a capital campaign or an upcoming missions effort. When you already have these tools in place you become much more nimble in your ability to respond quickly and remotely.

Imagine for just a moment that your community experiences a natural disaster and your church is already known in the community as a group that responds quickly and effectively to mobilize volunteers and financial resources. Along with other communication efforts, your church could send a group text message along with instructions for volunteering or providing financial support for relief aid. If you are respected and trusted in the community, you would be able to offer your *text giving* short code as a way for others outside your church family to get involved.

Crowdfunding

Crowdfunding can be an effective way to partner with people outside your normal sphere of influence to raise money for a specific project that benefits a person or group of people outside your congregation. Utilizing a personal fund-raising website like GoFundMe.com gives you access to people literally everywhere who look for humanitarian causes to support. This type of fund-raising will not likely be effective to secure funds that only benefit your congregation. But if your church is typically quick to respond to help those outside your community of faith, *crowdfunding* as a resourcing alternative can be effective. For a *crowdfunding* effort to be maximized you need to connect donors to a personal story and explain in detail what their gift will accomplish. People who fund these types of projects are committed to having an impact, so they will want to know how their gift makes a difference. Potential donors are most likely to participate using a *mobile device*, which forces you to be compelling in a concise manner. Build your site for a mobile platform; then modify it for a desktop screen size.

> If your church is typically quick to respond to help those outside your community of faith, *crowdfunding* as a resourcing alternative can be effective.

Receiving Payments for Goods and Services

Payments for goods and services—such as a book from the church bookstore, a small group resource, a vacation Bible school T-shirt, or a ticket to the Wednesday evening meal—are not tax deductible and therefore don't require the posting of a contribution. However, some of the same tools mentioned in this book, such as a mobile tablet or phone with a **card reader** or a text sent from a mobile phone, can make it extremely convenient to pay for church-related transactions if you are set up to offer them! Using electronic tools for broader applications helps people become more comfortable with them. As you continue persistent use and exposure, you will alleviate objections, build trust, and grow participation.

Eventually a leader will challenge a church to change the way it has always done things. Not just any leader, but an effective one. Not just change for the sake of change, but change for the sake of the church's impact or survival. Your church might be the one trying to use your edges in my skiing metaphor, and you might be the leader. I hope that someday the success story of the church in the following paragraphs might have similarities to the story of Your Church.

Success Story

Your Church could really be almost any church, located almost anywhere in the United States. Your Church doesn't care as much about how things get done as long as they get done. Your Church is primarily concerned with the Great Commandment and the Great Commission. Your Church doesn't care which person, or even which church, gets the credit; they just want the next person to experience the life-changing love and grace of God. Resourcing ministry is viewed as mission-critical work.

Your Church understands the way young families view stewardship is changing. It also believes that a culture of generosity can and should be developed. Your Church is looking for creative ways not only to teach people about tithing but also to provide them with tools to follow through on their hearts' desire to grow as disciples. Your Church is always looking for an edge, an opportunity to compete for discretionary giving over and above the tithe. Your Church believes their mission, their cause, is always worth considering.

This year Your Church will host a community fundraiser to help area children with food insecurity. Previously only area nonprofits would have had the vision and tools to make an event like this possible, but Your Church had run a smaller but similar fund-raiser within the congregation for youth camp last spring. In doing so they recognized the opportunity to make a greater impact and be instrumental in shaping the way Christianity is viewed in a community.

They will set a huge goal and leverage relationships that have been built with community leaders to host a gala where tens of thousands of dollars will be raised. The venue will be away from Your Church campus and the name of Your Church won't be splashed on the T-shirts. Donated items from local artists and vendors will be auctioned and paid for on-site. Awards will be presented to individuals who used social media ***crowd-***

funding efforts in the preceding weeks to kick-start the effort. The culmination of the evening will be a live *screencasting* event where attendees can text pledges and matching gifts during the event, with progress toward the goal being broadcast in real time. Digital tools will play an essential role in achieving success.

Chapter 7

Measure What Matters

Knowing Is Always Better than Guessing

I've heard him say it dozens of times to now thousands of people: "Knowing is always better than guessing" is a statement that Clif Christopher rarely misses an opportunity to share with a group gathered to hear him teach on the topic of stewardship. The statement has a broad application and is a constant reminder to me that we measure what matters. For many churches what matters are budgets, butts (in worship services), and baptisms. For other churches there are metrics for discipleship that use involvement in Christian education, small groups, or volunteerism as an indication of personal spiritual health or growth. Still other churches may have a system of classes that helps them guide people through steps to deepen their faith and commitment. These churches track the numbers of people who are engaging in each step and track the progress being made by individuals in order to keep encouraging them. While none of these measurements are the magic button for making disciples, the intention is to make discipleship a priority.

Likewise, if you plan to make a ministry initiative a priority, you should have some way to determine if you are allocating resources in an effective way. An electronic giving initiative should be expected to justify the resources committed to it, just like every other ministry in your church.

> An electronic giving initiative should be expected to justify the resources committed to it, just like every other ministry in your church.

Establish Baselines

Begin by determining what metrics will be beneficial for your ongoing assessment and then find out exactly where your current performance is for that metric. If this is your first effort to engage the congregation in electronic giving, it may be that this will be the genesis of data collection in some areas. If so, your baseline could be "zero" in a given metric. For other areas, you should have recent historical data that would provide an understanding of your starting point.

Suggested Metrics

Here is a list of suggested metrics that you should consider as you evaluate the effectiveness of your electronic giving engagement level in the congregation and its impact on your ministry resourcing:

- One-time or periodic electronic contributions in each of the following channels (average number of monthly users, average dollars per month, percent of total monthly contributions):

  - *Website*
  - *Kiosk*
  - *Card reader*
  - *Mobile*

- *Recurring* electronic contributions in each of the following channels (average number of monthly users, average dollars per month, percent of total monthly contributions):

  - *ACH* or *auto-draft*
  - *Bill pay* or *e-check*

- Additional metrics you should be tracking:

  - Overall electronic one-time and periodic users versus *recurring* users
  - Total electronic contributions (from all channels)
  - Percent of budget contributions given electronically
  - Percent of total contributions given electronically (includes designated giving)
  - Quarter-over-quarter (January–March last year versus this year, etc.) budget contributions (not just total income)

- Year-over-year budget contributions (not just total income)
- Total and new giving units (recommended threshold of $200/year to be considered a giving unit)
- Donor universe (all donor households in a given period/year)
- Per-worshipper contributions (yearly contributions divided by average worship attendance)
- Median annual gift
- The number of thank-you notes being sent by the pastor and staff in a given period

The Right Questions and Systems

There are systems or processes that need to be in place so that you can answer the right questions and generate more occurrences of a desired result. This is very simplified strategic planning. Your team needs to decide what questions reinforce your desired outcomes, and then someone on your team needs to be responsible for helping the team work toward the outcome. Here are some questions to get you thinking:

- What caused a person to make a first-time gift? When did a new giving unit begin?
- Why did someone move from one-time or periodic contributions to *recurring* contributions?

- How many clicks are required for someone to make a gift to our ministry through our website? How do we lower that number?
- How is a thank-you generated?
- What is an appropriate thank-you for _____ ?
- When we send an appropriate thank-you, how often does the donor make another gift within a given period?
- What happens to the giving pattern of someone who has completed our personal finance ministry course?

A Final Thought

Remember that you aren't alone in helping people make this transition to the use of digital media. Businesses and non-profits that the people in your congregation encounter every day are exposing them to opportunities to make transactions electronically. They realize that their success, and likely their existence, depends on building loyalty, developing customers and donors that keep coming back for their goods and services, and creating *recurring* transactions. They are investing megabucks to make sure they are effective. Pay attention to what they are doing and the messages they are using. Learn from their experience, and improve your own communication efforts. You aren't selling anything, but you are securing resources for the most important cause that exists. It's worth doing well so you can grow ministry!

Notes

1. Why and Why *Now?*

1. Karl Zinsmeister, *The Almanac of American Philanthropy* (Washington, DC: Philanthropy Roundtable, 2016), 1132; see also "Statistics," Philanthropy Roundtable, http://www.philanthropyroundtable.org/almanac/statistics/; *The 2014 U.S. Trust Study of High Net Worth Philanthropy*, U.S. Trust and Lilly Family School of Philanthropy, October 2014, http://newsroom.bankofamerica.com/files/press_kit/additional/2014_US_Trust_Study_of_High_Net_Worth_Philanthropy.pdf.

2. J. Clif Christopher, *Not Your Parents' Offering Plate* (Nashville: Abingdon Press, 2015), 2.

2. Plan Your Trip

1. *Wikipedia*, s.v. "Automated Clearing House," last modified August 21, 2016, https://en.wikipedia.org/wiki/Automated_Clearing_House.

2. "Automated Clearing House (ACH)," Bureau of the Fiscal Service, last updated December 17, 2014, https://www.fiscal.treasury.gov/fsservices/instit/pmt/ach/ach_home.htm.

3. *Wikipedia*, s.v. "Online banking," last modified August 24, 2016, https://en.wikipedia.org/wiki/Online_banking.

4. *Dictionary.com*, s.v. "kiosk," accessed August 26, 2016, http://www.dictionary.com/browse/kiosk?s=t.

5. *Wikipedia*, s.v. "Merchant account," last modified July 13, 2016, https://en.wikipedia.org/wiki/Merchant_account.

6. *Wikipedia*, s.v. "Mobile app," last modified August 22, 2016, https://en.wikipedia.org/wiki/Mobile_app.

7. *Wikipedia*, s.v. "Smartphone," last modified August 23, 2016, https://en.wikipedia.org/wiki/Smartphone.

3. Ski School
1. Used with permission.

5. Blues
1. Presented by Steve MacLaughlin, contributed by Chuck Longfield and Jim O'Shaughnessy, "Charitable Giving Report: How Nonprofit Fundraising Performed in 2015," *Blackbaud*, February 2016.

CPSIA information can be obtained
at www.ICGtesting.com
Printed in the USA
LVOW04s1045011216
515210LV00004B/4/P